W9-BTZ-867

Apples
for Everyone

BY JILL ESBAUM

Apples

For Natalie

Published by the National Geographic Society
1145 17th Street N.W.
Washington, D.C. 20036-4688

Library of Congress Cataloging-in-Publication Data

Esbaum, Jill.
 Apples for everyone / Jill Esbaum. -- 1st ed.
    p. cm.
 ISBN 978-1-4263-0523-8 (pbk. : alk. paper)
 1. Apples--United States--Juvenile literature. I. Title.
 SB363.2.U6E83 2009
 634'.11--dc22

                              2009012719

Printed in USA

13/WOR/3

Seen any apples lately?

Early each year, in orchards and backyards, apple trees bloom.

Drawn by the sweet smell, bees buzz from blossom to blossom.

As time passes, petals flutter to the grass, and fuzzy bumps appear.

Slowly the baby apples grow bigger, turning all shades of red.

A glowing green. A cheerful yellow.

Apples might have golden speckles or snazzy stripes.

Be round as a ball or tall and lumpy-bottomed.

Limbs droop, heavy with ripe fruit.

Some apples thud to the ground, then rot and become food for the growing tree.

At last it's fall—harvest time!—
and fresh apples are everywhere.

Grocery stores. Farmer's markets. Roadside stands.

You might even climb a ladder to pick your own.

Your teeth sink in—crunch!—and tart-sweet juice dribbles down your chin.

People bob for apples at Halloween parties or dip them into melted caramel for a sweet gooey treat.

Apples may be baked into pies and cinnamony desserts or added to a yummy Thanksgiving stuffing.

Some are cooked into thick applesauce or crushed to make juice.

On a chilly night, a steaming mug of tangy cider chases away goosebumps.

Apple trees have been growing in America for hundreds of years—since colonists brought pips, or apple seeds, from England.

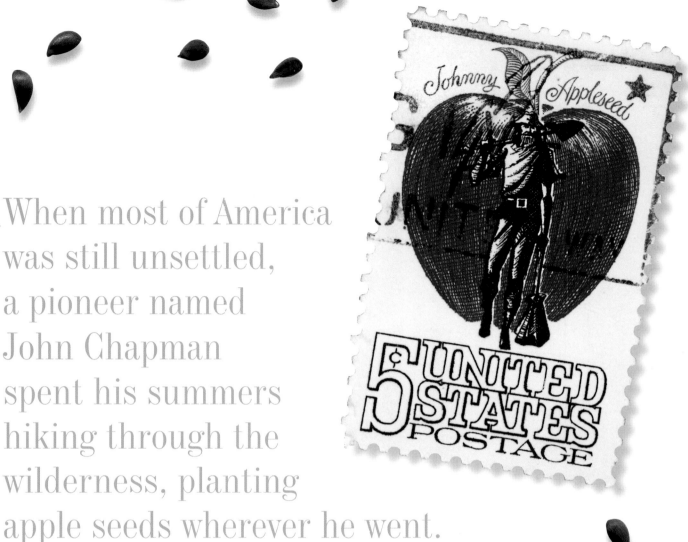

When most of America was still unsettled, a pioneer named John Chapman spent his summers hiking through the wilderness, planting apple seeds wherever he went.

His nickname was Johnny Appleseed.

An apple's seeds lie in its core. Cut an apple crosswise and you'll see the shape of a star.

Each of the star pockets has one or two seeds sleeping inside.

Americans eat
more apples than
any other fruit.

There are many flavors to choose from, with names like Fuji, Gala, Granny Smith, Honeycrisp, Jonathon, McIntosh, Pink Lady, and Red Delicious.

Have *you* found your favorite?

Ahh,
love at first bite!

Published by the National Geographic Society

John M. Fahey, Jr., *President and Chief Executive Officer*

Gilbert M. Grosvenor, *Chairman of the Board*

Tim T. Kelly, *President, Global Media Group*

John Q. Griffin, *Executive Vice President; President, Publishing*

Nina D. Hoffman, *Executive Vice President; President, Book Publishing Group*

Melina Gerosa Bellows, *Executive Vice President, Children's Publishing*

Prepared by the Book Division

Nancy Laties Feresten, *Vice President, Editor in Chief, Children's Books;* Bea Jackson, *Director of Design and Illustrations, Children's Books;* Amy Shields, *Executive Editor, Series, Children's Books;* Jennifer Emmett, *Executive Editor, Reference and Solo, Children's Books;* Carl Mehler, *Director of Maps;* R. Gary Colbert, *Production Director;* Jennifer A. Thornton, *Managing Editor*

Staff for This Book

Becky Baines, *Project Editor;* James Hiscott, Jr., *Art Director/Designer;* Lori Epstein Renda, *Illustrations Editor;* Grace Hill, *Asst. Managing Editor;* Lewis R. Bassford, *Production Manager;* Susan Borke, *Legal and Business Affairs*

Manufacturing and Quality Management

Christopher A. Liedel, *Chief Financial Officer;* Phillip L. Schlosser, *Vice President;* Chris Brown, *Technical Director;* Rachel Faulise, *Manager*

Original design by Molly Leach

1, Michael Edwards/ Photonica/ Getty Images; 2 top, Stock Connection/ Jupiter Images; 2 bottom right, Stephen Dalton/ Minden Pictures; 2 bottom left, Natasha Litova/ iStockphoto.com; 3 top, Nigel Cattlin/ Photo Researchers, Inc.; 3 center, Radius Images/ Jupiter Images; 3 bottom, Dyudin Stanislav Valer'evich/ Shutterstock; 4 top, SIME s.a.s/ eStock Photo; 4 bottom left, Biosphoto/ NouN/ Peter Arnold; 4 bottom right, Becky Hale/ NationalGeographicStock.com; 5 top, George Rose/ Getty Images; 5 bottom, Peter Clark/ Shutterstock; 6, John Marshall/ www.johnmarshallphoto.com; 7 top left, Chuck Nacke/ ipnstock.com; 7 top center, Mark Katzman/ Halo Images; 7 top right, Norm Eggert Photography; 7 bottom left, H. Reinhard/ Peter Arnold, Inc.; 7 bottom right, Emilia Stasiak/ iStockphoto.com; 8 left, Heather Perry/ NationalGeographicStock.com; 8 top right, Handke-Neu/ zefa/ Corbis; 8 bottom right, Jay Ahrend/ FoodPix/ Jupiter Images; 9 top, Michael Nichols/ NationalGeographicStock.com; 9 bottom, ipnstock.com; 10, Martial Colomb / Photodisc/ Getty Images; 11 top, Ray Roper/ iStockphoto.com; 11 bottom, John Kaprielian/ Photo Researchers, Inc.; 12, Snezana Negovanovic/ iStockphoto.com; 13, AAGAMIA/ Iconica/ Getty Images; 14-15, Jesus Cervantes/ Shutterstock; 14 top, Joel Sartore/ NationalGeographicStock.com; 15 top, Masterfile; 16, Masterfile; Cover, Polka Dot Images/ Jupiter Images.

For more information, please call 1-800-NGS LINE (647-5463) or write to the following address:

National Geographic Society
1145 17th Street N.W.
Washington, D.C. 20036-4688 U.S.A.

Visit us online at www.nationalgeographic.com/books
For librarians and teachers: www.ngchildrensbooks.org
More for kids from National Geographic: kids.nationalgeographic.com

For information about special discounts for bulk purchases, please contact National Geographic Books Special Sales: ngspecsales@ngs.org

For rights or permissions inquiries, please contact National Geographic Books Subsidiary Rights: ngbookrights@ngs.org

Brand new from National Geographic's
Picture the Seasons

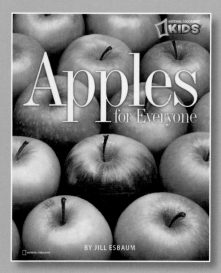

NATIONAL GEOGRAPHIC KIDS

Apples
for Everyone

BY JILL ESBAUM

ISBN: 978-1-4263-0523-8

NATIONAL GEOGRAPHIC KIDS

Seed, Sprout,
Pumpkin,
Pie

BY JILL ESBAUM

ISBN: 978-1-4263-0582-5

And don't forget your other Picture the Season favorites

NATIONAL GEOGRAPHIC SOCIETY

A Tree for All
Seasons

BY ROBIN BERNARD

ISBN: 978-0-7922-6674-7

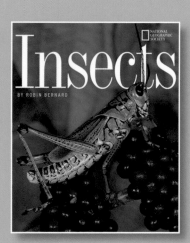

NATIONAL GEOGRAPHIC SOCIETY

Insects

BY ROBIN BERNARD

ISEN: 978-0-7922-6670-9

NATIONAL GEOGRAPHIC SOCIETY

Pilgrims
of Plymouth

BY SUSAN E. GOODMAN

ISBN: 978-0-7922-6675-4

NATIONAL GEOGRAPHIC

National Geographic's net proceeds support vital exploration, conservation, research, and education programs.

US $5.95 / $6.99 CAN

ISBN 978-1-4263-0523-8 / PRINTED IN USA

50595

9 781426 305238